ABACUS OF LOSS

ABACUS OF LOSS

A Memoir in Verse

SHOLEH WOLPÉ

The University of Arkansas Press
Fayetteville
2022

ISBN: 978-1-68226-198-9
eISBN: 978-1-61075-765-2

26   25   24   23   22   5   4   3   2   1

Manufactured in the United States of America

Designed by Liz Lester

Line drawings by Edvarda A. Braanaas (www.edvarda.art)

♾ The paper used in this publication meets the minimum
requirements of the American National Standard for Permanence
of Paper for Printed Library Materials Z39.48-1984.

Library of Congress Cataloging-in-Publication Data

Names: Wolpé, Sholeh, author.
Title: Abacus of loss: a memoir in verse / Sholeh Wolpé.
Description: Fayetteville: The University of Arkansas Press, 2022. |
  Summary: "In Sholeh Wolpé's memoir in verse, the poet wields an
  abacus as an instrument of remembering. Bead by bead, she takes
  the reader on a journey of love and exile, loss and triumph"—
  Provided by publisher.
Identifiers: LCCN 2021029515 (print) | LCCN 2021029516 (ebook) |
  ISBN 9781682261989 (paperback) | ISBN 9781610757652 (ebook)
Subjects: LCSH: Wolpé, Sholeh. | Poets, American—21st century—
  Biography. | Iranian American authors—Biography. | Iranian
  American women—Biography. | LCGFT: Autobiographies. |
  Autobiographical poetry.
Classification: LCC PS3623.O5935 A23 2022 (print) | LCC PS3623.
  O5935 (ebook) | DDC 811/.6—dc23/eng/20211213
LC record available at https://lccn.loc.gov/2021029515
LC ebook record available at https://lccn.loc.gov/2021029516

For my love, Eddie

The abacus is an instrument of remembering.

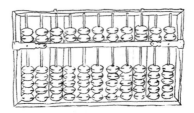

Pain is inevitable. Suffering is optional.

HARUKI MURAKAMI

CONTENTS

ACKNOWLEDGMENTS

My gratitude to the following publications where versions of these poems have appeared:

JOURNALS

Poetry London, Ambit Magazine, Consequence Magazine, The Chattahoochee Review, The Markaz Review, The Punch Magazine, Speak: The Magazine, Enchanted Verses Literary Review, Catamaran, National Poetry Library, UK, Patrik, Protrepsis: Revista de Filosofía, Mexico, Terrain: A Journal of the Built and Natural Environments, Levure Littéraire, and *Guernica: A Magazine of Arts and Global Politics.*

ANTHOLOGIES

The Ordinary Chaos of Being Human, edited by Marguerite Richards (Penguin Random House SEA, 2020); *Choice Words: Writers on Abortion,* edited by Annie Finch (Haymarket Books, 2020); *The Heart of a Stranger,* edited by André Naffis-Sahely (Pushkin Press, 2019); *Dear America,* edited by Simmons Buntin, Elizabeth Dodd, and Derek Sheffield (Trinity University Press, 2020); *Ink Knows No Borders,* edited by Patrice Vicchione and Alyssa Rayond (Seven Stories Press, 2019); *The Same Gate: A Collection of Writing in the Spirit of Rumi,* edited by Christopher Merrill and Natasa Durovicova (Autumn Hill Books, 2018); *Making Mirrors: Writing/ Righting by and for Refugees,* edited by Becky Thompson and Jehan Bseiso (Interlink Publishing Group, 2018); and *Before Infinity Ends,* edited and translated by Radek Hasalik (PEN in Czech Republic, 2015).

ABACUS OF LOSS

١

Color of Loss

I sit at this kitchen table in Los Angeles and take account: There
is my childhood house becoming smoke, friends scattered like
storm-blown dandelion seeds, my mother tongue ripped blue
from my throat.

See the man I used to call husband sinking into the twin lungs
of an ice beast, a love murdered by his own pallid hands;
see vein shades of lovers who came and went, a homeland
community in jail, my cousin's husband graying on the run,
my school principal and his wife hanging from beryl ropes.

> That we choose the color
> of our loss, like a blue
> sash draped across
> mourners' black. That
> eyes follow blind
> towards the cobalt moon,
> will slant us over and
> down, crooked toward
> mud on our graves.

چشم من آبی   روی من آبی   موی من آبی   خون من آبی   فکر من آبی   روح من آبی   آه من آبی   دست من آبی

خون من آبی   جای من آبی   زبان من آبی   چشم من آبی   روی من آبی   فکر من آبی   روح من آبی   موی من آبی

فکر من آبی   روی من آبی   موی من آبی   خون من آبی   چشم من آبی   روح من آبی   آه من آبی   دست من آبی

موی من آبی   جای من آبی   زبان من آبی   چشم من آبی   روی من آبی   فکر من آبی   روح من آبی   خون من آبی

روح من آبی   روی من آبی   موی من آبی   خون من آبی   فکر من آبی   چشم من آبی   آه من آبی   دست من آبی

زبان من آبی   جای من آبی   موی من آبی   چشم من آبی   روی من آبی   فکر من آبی   روح من آبی   خون من آبی

آه من آبی   روی من آبی   موی من آبی   خون من آبی   فکر من آبی   روح من آبی   چشم من آبی   دست من آبی

جای من آبی   زبان من آبی   چشم من آبی   روی من آبی   فکر من آبی   روح من آبی   موی من آبی   خون من آبی

Bead 2

Loss is a language
we all speak well,
a body moan that echoes
between ribs, the downfall
that becomes windfall.

Bead 3

Granddaddy takes me and my brothers out every Friday to a
circus filled with tigers, elephants, horses, and shirtless men in
glittering tights. There are women tinier than my child's body,
animals bigger than my room. It is roaring fun until the giant
with four faces. My arms begin to shake. Shivers ripple to the
tips of my fingers. Granddaddy puts a hand on my shoulder,
says: *It's just a mask on his head.*

But I know better

> because anything that's loved—
> a delicious granddaddy day
> in that circus in Tehran,
> sticky cotton candy melting
> its pink song into my mouth,
> my brothers, each naughty, toothy with joy—
>
> is always burning toward
> a future not yet come,
> fireworks in my brain,
> hot sparks welded to each memory.

Bead 4

A painted cardboard car
gives birth to
clown after clown.

Like lovers: the soldier, the thief, the cheater, the psycho lawyer.

Bead 5

Teacher says: List seven pleasures of life. His mustache is a street cat's tail. His index finger cuts the air. He says: Think morally, philosophically, and poetically, screeching his shoes along the narrow aisle between our desks.

Goli is teacher's pet. She gets everything *right*. Her name is called. She stands up and unwrinkles her uniform. Her pleasure list swims with God, with angels, goodness, and love.

I bite the insides of my cheeks.

When it's my turn, when I get to number 3, teacher inhales a noisy lungful of air and bangs his ruler on my desk.

Now, outside the principal's office, I roll up my left sleeve to hide a pomegranate stain. I watch the short-sighted secretary wrinkle her nose as she hammers an ancient typewriter. This is my third time in this chair.

I look at my list, again. It's a good list. An honest list. The best list in the whole city. Moses had his ten commandments. This is my seven.

Bead 6

Seven pleasures:

1. Sneak up to the rooftop while everyone sleeps and star-tan in your underwear while talking to God.

2. Pee in the rain gutter when Ahmad the bully passes by. He deserves every drop.

3. Peek through keyholes, anywhere, anytime. What's on the other side is always more interesting.

4. Scout the upper dining room cupboards for the raisin cookies Mama buys from Imperial Bakery on Amir Abad Street.

5. Dance in a mosque. But be prepared to die right after.

6. When shaking hands with the boy you like, sneak your phone number into his sweating palm.

7. Say no when all they want is yes.

٢

This Coffin

Bead 1

I lie on my old spring bed, thinking about girls who slit their
wrists; who pour kerosene on their heads and light a match.
I'll be thirteen soon.

> We kiss
> the warm earth,
> lips drawing
> moans from the sea.

> Like ghosts in flimsy shrouds
> fountains of semen
> re-create us
> sinew by shadow by flesh.

> And this coffin?
> Mine.

Bead 2

Mama's cousin is soon to be married. She's visiting from her village and they've installed her in my room. I ask about her fiancé. She says you're too young for that talk. Every night she shoves my doll into my arms and kisses me goodnight. Who takes comfort from sleeping with a stiff Mattel-made plastic body? If I tell her this, her eyelashes will blink away my words. I clutch the doll and say goodnight.

> Billboards retch
> meandering slogans, strike
> eyes with guns
> clutched by fetching rough men.
> Gone are the Marlboro cowboys
> roping their cattle, half-smoked
> cigarettes dangling from mouths.

Bead 3

I'm on a hill high above Tehran. Below, the city is veiled with
smog. I take a deep breath and walk down into the gray mass.
When I return, I write what I have seen. In one story, a girl is
stolen by a monster who hides her in a cave and loves her until
she catches his monster-ness like a cold. In another, a boy whose
schoolmates call him *najes*, unclean, takes revenge by spitting
into their Coke bottles when they are not looking. I have fifteen
such stories. I submit one to a contest at school and win. I show
Mama and Daddy the medal and read them the story; they smile
and say: *Bah-bah*, good job. When I tell them I have many more,
they say, *Go do your homework, it's almost dinnertime.*

> The house is corpses of women
> cooking meal after meal.
> The house is my voice
> trapped beneath blue bedsheets.
> It is a child on a rooftop watching
> stars, those scorching bodiless
> heads, shoot across night sky.
>
> My country stands behind a tree
> laden with fruit, yet hungry.
> Instead of seeds it plants
> landmines in the fertile soil;
> arranges vowels along
> its windowsills like shells
> from an oil-ridden shore.
>
>   I carry my coffin on my back.

Bead 4

I contemplate opening my veins with Mama's kitchen knife. I ask the poster of Googoosh, my pop rebellious idol: What's the point? Would my death cancel the wedding they are planning? Will it stop all jolly feasts in the family this year? Next year? Will they sing at my funeral? Googoosh narrows her eyes, lifts up her chin and says: Wear a red dress, will you?

> This city chokes in morning glory
> which grows along its tall windows
> over the tables and chairs of restaurants
> through the crevices of brick walls in old libraries.
>
> At the border stations they fill up
> our tanks with
> shoes and nightmares.

Bead 5

I have perfected the art of eavesdropping. I hide behind
furniture. Crawl under Mama's bed. Listen to adults. The
skeleton keyhole of my bedroom door opens to the living
room. I stick into it a long straw taped to heavy paper
rolled into an ear trumpet.

At night, the adults bring out baklava and tea. They huddle
around the bubbling samovar and talk. Our walls are thick. So
they don't whisper. Mama talks as if she's swallowed the school
principal's loudspeaker. She claims she is deaf in one ear because
my father snores like an elephant. I say, *Elephants don't snore.* She
points at Daddy and says, *This one does.*

Now I hold my breath and listen. But they are not speaking
about a marriage. They are not laughing. Panic like smoke
enters through the keyhole. Who has been arrested?

> Fear rocks the cradle until the city falls silent.
> It licks the inky outlines of churches
> and temples from its lips;
> the shadows of unbelievers and infidels.

> Doors uproot themselves.
> Want some ash for your soup?
> A little for your lover's tea?
> I promise, I will not haunt you.
> This is only to cure
> us. Of our names.

Bead 6

In Trinidad, my aunt takes care of me. My grandmother cooks
and gives plenty of advice. I get fat. My skin isn't dark enough.
It isn't white enough. My hair doesn't curl tight nor does it drop
straight like a waterfall. I wish I could iron my tongue, crease it
sharp so I could belong.

> Women sing absence like opera.
> They sprinkle it on white sheets like perfume,
> graft it to trees like branches from homeland,
> indelible scarifications on their lips.

> The dance is this late breeze,
> swings the hangman's rope.
> Cold fingers through my hair.

Bead 7

Daddy sends me to an all-girls boarding school in England. My roommate has long blonde hair. She mocks the dark hair above my lips. I buy tweezers. Mama's cousin calls, says the Basij came knocking on our door looking for her husband. He ran out the back door, thank God. But they would not leave empty-handed. They went next door and arrested our pregnant Bahá'í neighbor.

I want my Mattel doll back. I want it shoved into my arms. I promise not to eavesdrop.

> Refugees trail the narrow roads
> like sheep wandering edges
> of hallucination.
> They have no names, and their throats
> are foggy with mournful songs.
> They are the dead who smell of bone-ash.
> They carry their coffins on their backs
> and the bones in their eyes ache.

Bead 8

Think of those left behind, he says. *The young girls they just hanged—for refusing to convert.* A good religious girl, I'm on display under a bell jar. No boyfriends. No late-night parties. No drinking. In the United States of America, all Daddy cares about is protecting my virginity. He guards it like his wallet.

> Don't wish for death.
> It may hear you and come
> dressed like a clown.
>
> ·
>
> Don't wear your scars like notes
> scribbled in the margins of books.
> Don't line your shoes along the cold wings
> of a plane about to take off.
>
> Fear licks my living skin like a lynx.
> I walk with a coffin on my back.

Bead 9

To escape Daddy's rules, I get married. He is relieved. It's
exhausting to protect a girl in a place like America. He holds
his head between his palms when Mama reminds him of
what we have lost. The losing never stops. Not just things.
Family. Neighbors. People we have known all our lives. Dr.
so-and-so is now a dishwasher at a diner in DC. The engineer
who built such-and-such bridge lays tiles in rich people's homes
in LA. My school principal and his wife . . . well, they just
disappeared.

Tonight, I lose the way to my next dream.

Like a candle in a paper boat
Daddy offers me to the sea.
I chant every prayer I know
but no mermaid takes pity
and returns to me my childhood.

My songs will not wake the moon's face,
the house-grass, snow, donkeys burdened with almonds.

Instead, the sound of knives
sharpens against darkness.

Instead, my blouse aches from this cold,
contagious absence.

Bead 10

For a girl like me, living at home with her conservative parents, the only way to have sex is to get married.

I pick the youngest of them. A few years older than me, he too is a virgin, alas! which makes our first night . . . well, a bit complicated.

Someone says: Think cucumber. Now, I'm a Persian girl, so of course I imagine a tiny Persian cucumber, the kind my mother chops, five or six at a time, and puts in our Shirazi salad. But this is America and a single cucumber is a rolling pin.

A man tells my husband: The first night is like slaughtering lamb—make it swift. Well, how to be swift with a clueless virgin is a conundrum my young husband does not solve that night.

The day after, at the customary lunch party, men eye me with playful ease. I can almost hear their thoughts: *Not a virgin anymore . . . eh?* They look me up and down to see how much I have changed from the night before, as if a man's penis is God's miracle rod, electricity and all.

I go to the bathroom and throw up in the mirror.

> It is years
> later when I taste a durian.
> It smells of that night: a mélange
> of onions and used gym socks.
> It tastes like his kisses: creamy
> garlic, caramel, whipped cream.

I eat the durian because I can,
because it is delicious, the way
throwing up is delicious after
a humiliating meal.

Bead 11

I divorce and marry again. I look for home under every rock,
inside every shirt, between pistachio shells, even in the smoky
cloud rising from kebabs cooking over hot coals. I am naïve. So I
have children. They teach me everything except the meaning of
home. And when they are gone, I run. Again.

There is no kitchen on that rooftop.
Here are the abandoned bicycles.
The colors you buried between walls.
This rush of a train over a crumbling bridge.

The hyacinths carry the stench of false spring,
its incessant comings and goings, like lovers—
the bandit wolf, the psychotic cat, that horny dog.

Come back, Sholeh the child.
Let me splash inside you again,
sit in you without fear of drowning.
Let me drink from you,
declare you my country,
defend you with my wounded knees,
make my curly hair your flag,
my ribs, your borders.

Bead 12

Lovers. They come and are ejected. The entertainer who steals;
the hallucinating attorney; the trumpet player with medals and
guns; the double-dealing psychologist. The sum of them is less
than zero. There is nothing left to subtract. Every spring, the tree
in the backyard regains its leaves, but the mockingbird returns
with the same damn song in his beak.

> It is raining heartbeats again
> between operatic war sirens
> and the high notes of falling bombs.
> Rain washing the cobblestones,
> of ink, blood,
> washing till only ash remains
> clinging to my coffin like mud.

Bead 13

There is nothing but a flickering universe. God, a reckless adolescent, hardwired hope into our neurons. Beauty opens its eyes and greets us with its sky. We spread open our arms even though we know the blue is a lie.

> Every day, I stand in front of a firing squad.
> Eyes tightly bound with a red kerchief,
> I think about my mortgage, the price of utilities,
> the color of their boots.
> I stand in my puddle and worry
> about my burial expenses.
> They aim, but do not shoot.

> I dedicate this poem to the coffin on my back.

٣

The World Grows
Blackthorn Walls

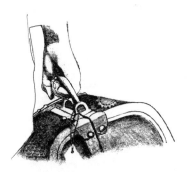

Bead 1

Tall, stiff and spiny.
Try to make it to the other side
and risk savage thorns.

We who left home in our teens,
children who crossed boundaries and were torn
by their thousand serrated tongues,
we who bear scars that bloom and bloom
beneath healed skins,
              who have we become?

I ask myself:
              Is home my ghost?
Does it wear my underwear
folded neatly in the antique chest
of drawers I bought twenty years ago,
nest inside my blouse that hangs
from one metal hanger I cannot discard?
Is it lost between these lines of books
shelved alphabetical in a language
I was not born to? Or here on the lip
of this chipped cup
my last lover left behind?

I carry seeds in my mouth. Plant
turmeric, cardamom, and tiny
aromatic cucumbers in this garden.
Water them with rain I wring
from my grandmother's songs.
They will grow, I know, against

these blackthorn walls.
They can push through anything, uncut.

I left home at thirteen.
I hadn't lived enough to know how
not to love.
Home was the Caspian Sea, the busy bazaars,
the aroma of kebab and rice, Friday
lunches, picnics by mountain streams.
                    I never meant to stay away.

They said come back
and you will die.

Exile is a suitcase with a broken strap.
I fill up a hundred notebooks with scribbles,
throw them into fire and begin again,
this time tattooing the words on my forehead,
this time writing only not to forget.

Complacency is catching like the common cold.
I swim upstream to lay my purple eggs.

They say draw sustenance from this land,
but look how my fruits hang in spirals
and smell of old notebooks and lace.

What is a transplanted tree
but a *time being*
who has adapted to adoption?

Spirits urge and spirits go,
they weep and wail at the door of the temple
where I sit at the edge of an abyss.
Perhaps it's only in exile that spirits arrive.

But even this is an illusion.

Bead 2

Dear America,
you used to creep into my room,
remember?

I was eleven and you kept coming,
night after night, in Tehran, slid in
from inside the old radio on my desk, past
the stack of geometry homework, across
the faded Persian carpet, and thrust
into me with rock and roll thumps.

I loved you more than bubble gum,
more than the imported bananas
street vendors sold for a fortune.

I thought you were azure, America,
and orange, sky and poppies,
like Mama's new dress, and kumquats.

I dreamed of you America, I dreamed
of you every single night with the ferocity
of a lost child until you became true like flesh.

And when I arrived,
you punched yourself into me
like a laugh.

Bead 3

Cat-shaped on the map, crowned
with a land-locked sea that collects
and drowns shooting stars.

Such optimism in 1979 Iran.

If only we had known what the whirlwind of turbans
hid within its folds—

> Children rushing into minefields, hands in pockets
> clutching golden keys to Heaven. Men on motorcycles
> slashing women's bare arms with poison razor
> blades. The Basij rushing *Midsummer Night's Dream*,
> arresting the director for *raping the public's innocence.*

I left you the way a body
tricks its shadow behind.
But shadows are masters
at following their makers.

۴

Please Stop

Bead 1

The day a wrinkled cousin put her hands on me and said she would teach me about men and their women, I said, *please, stop.*

The day a mustached waiter placed his palms on my young chest and rubbed as he helped me across the street, I said, *please, stop.*

The day a stranger danced his fingers under my skirt in a dark cinema when I was ten, I said, *please, stop.*

The day my boss closed the door to his office and felt my thighs under the cover of our working table, I said, *please, stop.*

The day an eminent Iranian scholar set his wine glass on the railing of a fence, grabbed my shoulders and pulled me in for a kiss, I pushed him back and said, *please, stop.*

The day a lover shoved me hard against the bedroom wall and bruised my wrists, I said, *please, stop.*

I have always been such a polite girl.

Bead 2

I don't want them, those spicy corpses washed
and fried, crickets caught at the moment of flight
like terrified citizens of Pompeii.

But it's a few drinks past noon and we are flirting, this man and I,
he, in high leather riding boots, three pedigree dogs by his side,
me, in flowing silk cinched tight around my waist.

The guests drink tequila, suck on quartered limes,
wander our host's plush garden this side of Cuernavaca,
hidden behind these ivy-crusted walls.

Again, I say no
to the handful of tiny bodies he holds before my lips.
They smell of chili and sparkle with crystal salt.

His teeth are an unbroken row of stiff cavalry
clad in faded white.
One, two, three.
Then, *See?* He laughs. *Not so bad.*

He pushes them into my mouth, says: *Swallow.*

Bead 3

The yellow daisies along the runway droop from thirst. I haven't
had my shot of espresso and the fellow next to me keeps staring
at my breasts.

> Last night, at the hour between night and dawn
> books grew feet they dangled from wooden shelves,
> the salt shaker on the kitchen table
> was an object from Andromeda,
> and the white lilies suddenly gagged
> on their own stamen tongues.

I close my eyes, pretend the man is a cockroach, but his stare
laser-burns my nipples, sets fire to the twin cities under this thin
purple blouse.

> Ghosts can be inhaled,
> secrets held between eyelashes,
> and the scent of light splashes carelessly
> across a naked body.

> Perhaps I don't love you anymore.

I pick up a book, hold it high in front of me. He shifts his body,
drops his head, then nervously twiddles his thumbs. When I
lower the book, his gaze returns to my chest.

> We break into tears and sweat
> just as easily as they break into us.
> It's like lighting a candle at noon.
> It's writing this poem with lemon juice.

I shift my body, look straight into his creeping blue eyes and prepare to stab him with my tongue.

> Madness is a sad song that repeats
> night's blue wisdom,
> its swollen confessions,
> its puckered mouth.

The man blinks and quickly says: *Please forgive me. I have OCD and won't be able to bear this long flight if that pin on your blouse remains unhooked.*

> The fastest way out of a labyrinth
> is up.

Bead 4

What do you do when the old kettle you've put on flames for tea begins to whimper like an injured bird?

A. Ignore it and drop your face back into your book.

B. Stare at it like the Pope has just dropped his pants.

C. Go outside and smoke a French cigarette. Never mind that you don't smoke.

D. Empty the kettle and examine the inside like a lunatic.

E. Remain in your kitchen chair and sob hysterically because that whimper was yours all along.

۵

(Un) Lovers

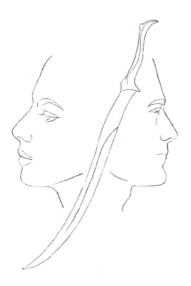

Bead 1

His breath is radioactive.
His Oxfords jik-jik on the slick

floors of the gallery like hungry birds
among frenetic landscapes of blue.

These endless canvases make me dizzy—
or is it his cologne stinging my brain?

His fingers brush the nape of my neck,
cup my bony shoulders in his palms.

White lines slash blacks on a square canvas,
ravage the base yellow into untidy rips.

Watching us from across the corridor:
Jesus on a digital cross.

Bead 2

He wraps the bedsheet around his naked waist,
goes to the window, lights a cigarette.

He smells of things distant: lemon groves,
almond blossoms and gun powder.

It is almost noon, and the sky has thrown
its searchlight on his shaved head.

A cool breeze investigates the scars
on his back. A truck passes by, releases its city smells.

He looks at me, says: *Habibti, it's time to go.*
I drown deeper into the mattress.

Someone turns on the radio next door.

Our passports lie on the yellow Formica table
side by side, two countries at war.

Bead 3

Yesterday I saw the ghost of a shark.
Today there was a tarantula in my hat.

I've come to Journey's End in Belize
with my mate of twenty years to salvage
what Mama calls our holy bond.

He says, Let's pray. I take off my clothes.
I say, Let's cha-cha. He pops a valium.

I've never had a pistachio, says the bartender.
Does it grow in a bush? He sucks out the salt,
spits the hard shell into my open palm.

I crack the shell like a vow,
place the meat on his tongue.

Bead 4

The moon is a bruised fist tonight.
It has obliterated the stars.

I sleepwalk across the tiny island
to you, *mi Hombre Sin Miedo*,
my stony love.

It's dark and the padre in the chapel
with his missing arm and chipped toes
is soaked in yellow holy halo.

But you, *mi amor*, my lichen-crusted
beloved, stand against this moon-lit wall,
eyes sewn to the sea. Such sadness
in the curve of your spine, the tilt of your neck.

Does the smell of death still reek
through the crevices of this blood-stained wall?

Do the cries of men in Franco's blizzard of lead
still echo in the chiseled chambers of your ears?

Here are my eyelashes.
Take them in your lips.

Here is my forehead.
Let it rest on your chin.

Here is my tongue.

Something behind the wall shudders and shakes
the ancient oak. Leaves flutter and rain.

We kiss like ghosts.

۶

Pink

Bead 1

She is still bleeding three days later, still in pain. We return to the clinic on the other side of town. Her feet are put back into the stirrups, her legs pulled apart. There are pieces still clinging to her womb like strands of red algae. The procedure has to be repeated.

No, no, she sobs, *I can't do it again.*

Bead 2

Mama used to call her "prime good." The way she blinked her green eyes and deepened her dimples, the way she swayed her hips and unbound her silky brown hair from a tight ponytail, triggered desire even in straight women.

> Now she lies on a cold hard bed,
> legs sprawled.
> She scrunches her face,
> bites her lower lip,
> lifts her shoulders and neck,
> and squeezes my hand so hard I want to scream.
>
> I brush away strands of hair from her eyes,
> this girl who was once the jewel of Tehran.

Bead 3

We met when we were eleven at a summer camp at the base of
Alburz Mountain. She came dressed in enviable jeans made in
the UK, I came armed with a new skit I had written and copied
in lined notebooks. We each wanted what the other had: I, her
exquisite beauty, and she, my easy wit.

> We folded into each other
> like a two-paper origami.

Boys I had a crush on, fell for her. It would be a lie to say it didn't
hurt. But beauty like that was a gift from God. So, I became the
chronicler of her tears, the dispenser of advice, the therapist,
the silly cheer-up clown.

Bead 4

Now, between her thighs,
the doctor is playing
a war game with her body's desire
to hold on to what has been imposed—
by nature, God, angels, chance.
What does it matter now?

Bead 5

Her Persian lover is doused with Paco Rabanne aftershave. He
sits in the clinic's spotless waiting room. They were once in love.
Or lust. He has two kids; she has one. He has a conservative
wife; she's divorced. He is ambitious; she is bitter about what life
has dealt her. Perspectives make any story playdough. You can
shape and tell it a hundred ways.

> Silence.
> Then the plop,
> the clink
> of metal against metal.

The doctor walks over to the counter, puts the bowl in the sink,
then leaves. His leather shoes suction the linoleum floor.

> I casually wander to the sink.
>   (Shouldn't have.)
> What's inside that metal bowl
> melts my marrow—
>
> not because it's gruesome,
> or violent,
> but because it's a nothing,
> just a slimy pink ooze.
>
> Is this how we begin?
> This?

Bead 6

She moans, *It hurts*. I don't know if she means her heart or her womb. I look away from the sink, and something catches fire between my eyebrows, a scalding ache like the sting of a scorpion. I pull a blanket over my friend. She closes her eyes. Her face is swollen. Lines around her eyes spread like runaway roads to nowhere.

Bead 7

He believed in skin to skin.
Pills nauseated her.
She imagined she was too old to sprout his seed.

Each time he brought her tuberoses
wrapped in golden cellophane.

Bead 8

I throw up my breakfast in the bathroom, yogurt and peaches that look like a whirling universe of pink starfish. The doctor comes back, asks my friend how she is feeling. She cries. I go to the waiting room and watch her lover pay the bill in cash. His wallet is black. He counts the bills one by one.

Bead 9

How is she? he asks.

I shrug.

He drops his head, shakes it east to west, west to east.

I do love her, he says.

His eyes are the color of burnt toast.

I rub the pain between my eyebrows, tell him, *She doesn't want to see you.* He nods, turns to leave then stops. *Tell her I'm sorry. For this. For everything.*

I want to say, *Tell her yourself, jellyfish.* But my tongue is suddenly stone.

Bead 10

She is dressed and ready to go. Walking is difficult. Living is difficult. Especially today.

> Shame is indelible.
> If you let it, it will stain
> your forehead like a tattoo.

The doctor puts his hand on her shoulder, pats it gently. He is like that steel bowl, he holds within himself what he yanks out. That is his sacrifice.

He looks at me, straight at me, and I know he's read my thoughts. Or maybe every friend who comes to hold hands has the same thought, this same grateful look. Maybe he registers us all in his eyes and stows us away in the vaults of his consciousness for the days when he battles fear, doubt or fatigue.

Bead 11

Her apartment smells of dead tuberoses. I tuck her in, make
her chicken soup. She wants a cigarette. I give her two. She
smokes five. Drinks tea. Refuses soup. I pick up her daughter
from school, buy her a new backpack. The girl is happy. Life is
that simple when you are nine. At Johnny Rockets, she mixes
ketchup and mayonnaise, spreads it on her burger. The same
shade of pink.

Bead 12

The doctor is scraping my friend's womb once more. I put my
hand on her shoulder and squeeze. She looks up at me and
suddenly she is as she was all those years ago at the summer
camp in Iran. I am struck by the powerful pull of her bright
green eyes. Beauty was not her blessing.

This is my punishment, she cries. *God is punishing me for my sins.*

> I want to say, God in whose garment?
> Under what mask?
> In what country and under what law?
> But this is not the time for religious quarrels.

> Instead,
> I pinch myself pink.
> The pain radiates, numbs
> my tongue so that the only sound
> I push out of my throat is a hushed desperate groan.

V

Faith

Bead 1

A blank page is not innocent
        because it is white.
Innocence is not
        blank.

Bead 2

Every summer day by the Caspian Sea, after a morning's salt water and sun, playing in the hot sand, then lunch and a nap in our villa, I skip from one end of the resort to the other for the only shop on the compound where I exchange my ten rials for a bag of cheese puffs and a bottle of Canada Dry orange soda.

My favorite spot is the resort's veranda adjacent to the restaurant. There, I lounge on a large chair stuffed with something soft, like bird feathers or sheep fleece. From here I can see the sea, measure its breath against my own.

> That day, the sweet-salt sea
> was agitated, as if
> the Russians on the other side
> were hunting waves
> on backs of seahorses and whales.

Earlier, Mama had blow-dried my long curly hair. It falls silky around my bony shoulders. I stare at the cover sketch of my new book, *Ivanhoe*. The young man, bare-chested and muscular, rides on a horse-drawn chariot, his whip held high in the air.

I bend over to rest my soda, and my fingers brush something sticking out from under the chair. It is a tattered, dusty English magazine, perhaps left behind by an American visitor. On its cover stands a man-rabbit dressed in suit and bowtie, leaning casually on one hip, a hand in his pocket, another holding a glass of champagne like the ones served to the adults at the resort's bar.

What a cute rabbit, I think. Small pictures surround him like exotic postage stamps. I look closer.

The pictures are of women. Their soccer-ball bottoms on high stools, pomegranate breasts cupped and offered.

Slowly, I turn the page.

Through my veins travels a kind of ecstasy only an eight-year-old can conjure. The fizzy liquid orange softens the cheese puffs' salty crunch and bonds my tongue to the roof of my mouth, then spreads itself slowly down my throat.

Bead 3

We're all trees, upright,
heading towards winter. Shedding
leaves is our fucking fate.

Bead 4

Sitting with three open books black with the meandering
calligraphy of a "terrorist language" at an American airport
is a terrible idea.

But five hours early, what's a girl to do but risk it, open what
she must under the watchful eyes of TSA and cameras that
blink when a person of unknown dark curly-hair origin is
spotted with undecipherable texts, possibly manuals for mass
destruction of something.

A few people pass by, too casually perhaps, and peek at the
books, but in the end, it's a sweeper who soft-shoes his way
towards me, a Latino Fred Astaire with fake bushy mustache.
He runs his broom to and fro, moving dust closer and closer to
my ridiculously high-heeled red shoes, then stops. He pretends
to notice me for the first time, puts his small chin on the stick of
his broom, gathers his mouth as if around a cut lemon, squints,
then asks in Spanish, *¿Que es esto? Greico?*

Good move, I think, so you no hablas Ingles, amigo. I look up
and give him a sly smile. He parts his lips, slightly. His teeth are
corn-yellow. A smoker for sure. But that mustache? It takes all
my strength to not reach up and pull. To see if it comes off.

I answer in Spanish, *No, this isn't Greek, it's Persian poetry.*

He lifts his chin, says, *¡Bien! ¡Hablas Español!* He then bends over
the book for a closer look. I say, this time in English, *Poetry*, and
point to the shape of the couplets. *See?* I say, *A line of Persian
poetry consists of two hemistiches separated like this.* I point to the

blank space between separated texts. He ungathers his lips from their concentrated pose, nods, mumbles something about how he hated memorizing poetry at school, then in perfect accentless English: *Don't miss your flight.*

With that, he turns on his heels and just as deliberately, soft-shoes back, towards some place, over there, broom still in hand, past a door that appears and disappears like an itch, scratched.

Bead 5

I say God is just a vagabond
peddling bombs and swords
and Daddy says he'll never speak to me again.

Aunt calls on the phone and monologues for hours.
Brothers shake their heads in disbelief.

They ask why, but my answer is in a tongue they refuse.
It is printed on a flag they do not recognize.

A mound of question marks allows greater oxygen
than periods and exclamation marks.

I tell Mama, *Look, I'm bathed in light.*
She says, *No, child, it's the Beloved leaving your soul.*

Bead 6

I tell Mama I am leaving religion and its foggy tales.
She points at the wall of books in my room,
says, *It's their fault.*

Bead 7

A tempest is brewing in my pen
from which the ink of an "infidel"
is about to spill and stain
the walls of faith.

The turbaned owls of the crescent moon
the robed bears of the cross who have painted
the sun on the limestone walls of this prison
set fire to the air we breathe.

God weeps behind the mask tattooed on its face.

Bead 8

The Beloved like the sun will gleam
The lover like an atom will spin
When love's spring zephyr begins to stream
Every branch not dead will begin to swing

A house of worship is just a place. That uplifting vibration is the pulse of the Beloved inside our veins—lover and beloved twined like the braid of our genes.

In the path of desire, the wise and the foolish are as one
In the ways of love, the friend and stranger are as one
Those gifted the wine of union with the beloved
In their creed, God's House and idol temples become as one

This is how I enter every mosque: with a covered body and a naked soul. I pray inside my eyes, inside the cave of my own being. I say words without the aid of breath, think thoughts with my spirit, and bow before no one.

Sometimes hidden and sometimes revealed am I
Sometimes a Muslim, a Christian or a Jew am I
To fit my heart into everyone else's heart
Each day someone other and new am I

I hum prayers under my breath, under every ravishing dome of each mosque, beneath its delicate beauty, among the souls of the artists who gave eyes, backs, hands and souls to its grandeur.

But here we huddle behind ropes and wooden barriers, on the periphery, the other side, covered head to toe. We kneel side by side, stand up in prayer, hold one another between the pillows of our hips.

The men pray freely, directly under the dome. This needles that dangerous part of me I call RED, because she *is* red—the wild-horse woman I strain to keep under check.

> At Shams-i-Tabrizi's tomb
> the mosque's wall-to-wall
> machine-made carpet is red.

> I break the rules, shun the women's
> section behind ropes, back and black,
> out of the way, sit against a wall beneath
> a large framed plaque of His name,
> the calligraphy like long entwined fingers
> of a goddess with endless golden nails.

Perhaps this is sacrilege, the wrong place to sit under His name. But no one looks, no one comes to gather and reprimand, to shoo this female to where she belongs, behind that rope, out of the way.

I watch the Pashtu poet among us, the dark man of religion in his customary white garb and black Western jacket. He smiles almost never, and watches everyone with eyes impossible to read. Someone says he is a Taliban.

He comes, comes towards me,
a dark coiling cloud,
stops short, then lifts up his long
arms and his suddenly beautiful
bearded face, in prayer.

Now certain I am sitting
where I must not, a blasphemy in red
beneath the Creator's entwined gilded name,
I gather my knees, hold them tight
like children in need of cheer and shield.

He bends and unbends,
lifts large palms up towards
the sky beyond this dome
where blue is light's repeating lie.

Outside: dusty roads, apricot fields,
sheep grazing in brown pastures,
olive trees lined up like rows of devoted
worshippers, rooted to the earth; to us.

Yesterday I reached for him with a Dervish greeting. This is
how: you take his hand, entwine it in your own, then kiss it,
and allow it to be kissed. Something in his eyes warned me to
not put my lips on his skin (so dark and soft), to not offer my
own hands to his lips (trembling).

Now, he mutters his holy words.
Sparrow song. Bows,
puts his forehead
to the ground, his hair
so black not even light
escapes the strands.

Watch him pull me into his
horizon, suck me
into his wormhole on the other
side of which he still
prays, except that here, in this
alternate universe,

he bows not before a god
but before *me*,
this female blinking danger,
soft, strong and RED,
refusing

his black, refusing his white.
RED who knows when to give,
what and how to take.
RED who is the explosion
in Shams, the dance in *sama*,
the music in Rumi's whirling words, a sky
on fire, the heart of the third planet,

even the curled strands of this carpet
on which a thousand praying men
lay their foreheads. RED,
the shawl on my head, on my soft,
naked arms, RED, the ink, the blood.

In this universe, my Pashtu friend, my fellow poet, you pray to
this, this immutable RED, the color that refuses.

∧ Honeymoon among Sargassum

Bead 1

Had your Mexican mother
met my Iranian, would
they have foretold us
in tea leaves? Seen us
in throats of blind bats
in caves, deep in Cenote Zancil-Ha,
luxuriant in our shade
of black, savage and supine?
Or in the cloudy discharge
that oozes from the cut
stem of an unripe fig?

Bead 2

They are digging deep holes in the sand, these men who will later bring us huevos rancheros on hot clay plates. Sometimes they lean on their shovels and look past the shore into the belly of the horizon, through which once upon a time Spaniards came and never left.

> Sweet as salt, pink as lazy pulse,
> immeasurable,
> biblical.
> Your finger in my mouth.

Bead 3

They speak Mayan, these beautiful men. The vowels drawn and
melodic, hammered by the throat in rhythmic beats.

> We sprinkle stolen holy water
> on our naked bodies in Tulum,
> transform them
> into unpronounceable charms
> that un-scar old wounds.

Bead 4

The holes are deep. They dig deeper. The sand is dawn-cold.
The breeze, wet. Who do you bury today?

> Yesterday in the park
> hungry crows gathered
> like spilled ink.
> They whipped the air
> into formation, like longing
> for fire,
> for you,
> down to my feet
> where ants flex their striated muscles.

Bead 5

Look, they say, and point to what the sea has brought in
overnight. An offering. Purposely severed from life. Piles of
brown, swollen corpses.

> This swelling tide
> breaks in drops of water
> that fall like sacrilegious sins
> over the furrowed brows
> of cultivated fields— this,
> your naked body next to mine.

Bead 6

The one with round cheeks and stubble on his chin says:
Sargassum. He pronounces it with flourish, lifts an armful
of the floating fronds named by the Portuguese sailors after
the Sargasso Sea. Robust, flexible. Piles of them browning the
stretch of platinum sand.

> I well know
> the exact measurement
> of your lips,
> the depth of your dimples,
> the width of your eyes,
> the circumference
> of your naval,
> the insistent curve
> of your midnight.

Bead 7

Give them back to the sea, I plead. The men shake their heads,
black with shiny hair. Shrug. *Muerte*, they say. The sea never
takes back the sacrifice.

> We are a shoreless lake, beloved,
> skirtless mountains, dirt roads
> to the end of nothing,
> roots that cling
> to the bottom of worn
> boats crusted with our stories.

Bead 8

The men gather the beached corpses, pile them high, those
long, swollen limbs, salty wet, all veins, gas-inflated, gleaming in
the rising red sun.

> This hunger;
> this space between this tongue
> and your lips.
> We disrobe and scale
> all the while never departing
> always entering one into another
> breaking between the notes
> of saxophone, oboe, violin.

Bead 9

In the Mayan ruins a hundred fifty kilometers west of these
shores a dry well harbors piles of bones. Sacrifices to whatever
gods were worshipped. The living roars like the sea.

> It was always so
> from the beginning,
> this lavish sky
> hidden behind a terrible storm,
> this runaway train
> that repeats itself
> in folds and unfolds of light.
> Desire is porous as thirst,
> cloudy as the inside of this coconut
> the mustached street vendor
> breaks for us with a smile.

Bead 10

The beach has been restored to its immaculate gold. The men have come in, washed, brewed our coffee, heated the stove for eggs.

> Your skin, this blade of grass smell, our
> repeating limbs from the sweat-soaked
> sheets, before daybreak's quick pulse,
> like the heartbeat of a frog. And there, too,
> buried sargassum . . . still, bleeding the sea.

٩

Un-Blinking Eyes

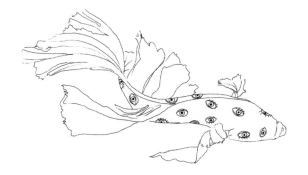

Bead 1

The day we lose my brother, I am six.

Daddy comes home loud as the Coca-Cola truck.
How do you lose a three-year-old?
Mama cries and pulls at her freshly curled hair.

The policeman says: *Check with the neighbors.*
We knock on every door, two streets up, five streets down.
Every time we hear a child cry,
Daddy's knees melt like ice cream,
Grandma crumbles like a cracker and waves her arms at God.

I go to the end of our garden, pull a chair out of the shed,
climb up and breath-whisper into my cupped palms.
I tell the birds: *Omid's missing. My little brother.*
Have you seen him? Help us find him please.

Finches flitter from branch to branch.
Doves coo from among the leaves.
Warblers fuss and consult.

And then it's like a silly cartoon.
My little brother emerges
from the back shed, a tiny barefoot bird
in diapers, covered head-to-toe
with feathers from Grandma's discarded quilt.

Bead 2

Niece,
I remember when they cut your mother
and pulled your sister out, then you,
and how you cried and cried.
You never wanted to be here.
Right from the start.

I open Mama's old prayer book
but the words billow like rain.
I wish you had loved
one thing enough to make you
want to stay; the orange sunsets,
your drooling dog, the fig tree
in the backyard, your twin sister's mole,
Cheerios in cold milk.

Washing your body now,
twenty-four years of bones and flesh
laid out tall and stiff on this hard table,
is the cruelest task.

I stand here full of heartbeat.
Touching you is like dipping hands in a cold sea.

I soak a porous sponge in water scented
with rose, brush it against your neck,
along your arms, those long, thin legs.
There is a tampon still inside, the string
hanging out like the detonator of a bomb.

Darkness bends over itself to devour
what it will not hold—
the boy you loved watched you cry,
take a handful of pills,

                and said nothing.

Bead 3

Is that my son they're rushing to, crushed like a can of beans in
his small Infiniti? Police cars, two ambulances, a tow truck.

I keep to the slow lane, ready to jump out, bulldoze the police,
scratch my way through the emergency crew, for his body, all
six foot six of Alex, there on the hot asphalt, shirt blushing with
blood.

But no.
Another mother's child.

> Later, as we eat my Mama's roasted
> beef, grilled tomatoes, and bowls
> of cool tangerine-scented pudding,
> Alex's face flashes: The new job at JPL,
> the girl from Russia he loves,
> the downtown apartment he wants to rent,
> the life he imagines he will forever live.

Bead 4

And I thought, perhaps Daddy was right.

At nine I imagined the dots
on our pet fish
as unblinking eyes, dark holes
that took in our distorted faces
through the sky of her plastic tank.

My brother's fingers made waves
in her world, sent her scurrying
behind the plastic grass, the way his pounding
kicks on my bolted bedroom door sent me
hiding behind my unsteady bookshelf,
chewing on long strands of my wild hair.

Every year, Daddy replaced the hole-ridden
bedroom door, until one day he didn't—
as punishment he said, because:
What do you do daughter to incite him so?

I began to conceal the kick marks and dents:
Magazine faces thick with makeup,
curvaceous bodies in short skirts holding up
a box of detergent, a tube of toothpaste,
their impeccable orthodontic smiles . . .
and I thought, perhaps Daddy was right—
my brother *was* always after something,
the marble I found and claimed, the bowl
of cherries I sequestered, or those records

I played on my red turntable, refusing
to share that corner
of joy carved from air,
mine alone. Then, now. Last night,
at Mama's house, after a meal

of lamb smothered in saffron sauce, potatoes
fried to a crisp, rice slippery with butter,
my brother wanted again. He kicked
with his words, called me whore
because I live with a man out of wedlock.

What is he after now? *Abroo?*
Honor, "clear water on the face" to blur sins
the way our courtyard pond hid its algae
imagining itself the nocturnal seat of the moon?

Or is my beloved brother
                              (and believe me, I love him)
after something I can never fathom,
universally virile— something
perhaps only a fish with a hundred
unblinking eyes may see?

Bead 5

Mama is upstairs blow-drying her curls. At eighty-five, her hair is still thick as eels, plentiful as a blessed wheat harvest. She rolls each section on a round brush, keeps it under heat until it steams like punishment. We are downstairs, Daddy and I. He sits on an old couch, cracking pistachio nuts.

There is a large piece of almond cake in my mouth when Daddy leans over, says: *Did you know I was crazy in love with another woman when I married your mama?*

His eyes are moonlighting in the well of their irises. I take a gulp of tea. It burns the lining of my throat. He lifts his thumb and forefinger to draw in the air the shape of her chin, the height of her cheekbones, the depth of dimples on her round cheeks.

I wonder where she is now, he mumbles more to himself than to me, then cracks open another nut, pops the salty kernel in his mouth and chews absentmindedly. His thin graying mustache rolls like a tiny wave.

I met her on a train, he says. *She got off in a village. The next week I rode the same train to the same station, got off and asked my way to her home. You could do that in those days in Iran. Their door was blue, peeling from neglect or poverty. I never forget how she looked in that pink dress. It was long but pinched at her waist, showing off her figure; three layers of white ruffles fell over her chest like this.* He surfs both hands the way a king waves at his subjects, then slides his gaze past the lemon tree outside to a place even more distant than memory.

She opened the door, he continues, *like she was expecting me; invited me to stay for lunch. Her mother spread a flowery vinyl tablecloth on the floor over which she laid out rice and eggplant stew, yogurt drink and cold melon.* He looks down and rubs the back of his hand. *They switched on the radio. Marzieh was singing. Her father said, "Bah-bah, welcome to our humble home." That's how they welcomed this tall, rich city boy . . . and why not?*

Daddy takes a deep breath and sinks into himself like a rusted ship. He is now in his own forgotten country on the other side of his thick glasses. He mutters: *I never went back. Didn't bother. Your grandfather would never have approved. Of her.*

So you gave up your love? I ask. *For family? Approval?*

The baritone-roar of hairdryer stops like the engine of a plane that has just arrived. Mama descends the narrow stairs like a queen in a fluffy blue robe. She says, *What are you two whispering about?*

It's not a question. She doesn't wait for an answer because she imagines there is nothing about Daddy she does not know. Not after fifty-five years. She shuffles in her slippers into the kitchen to make the evening's meal of rice and stew.

Mama is frying onions now. The sweet smell permeates the room with nostalgia. She hums to a tune in her head and I think: Mistakes are the sinews that hold our bones.

Daddy empties his plate of pistachio shells into the trash, switches on the TV, puts up his legs and before long he is snoozing into the rhythm of a game show.

١٠

The Tally

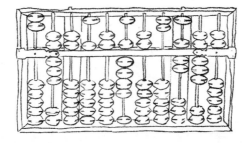

Bead 1

The moon rose bright and night drove us into dizzy exile.
Language became a desert with no name.

> In the end, friend, what is there to do
> but to continue to believe
> the same sun that burns away forests and skin
> gives prairies of daisies and groves of pears.

That night the lilies on Mama's table were her eyes. Sunbursts of
disbelief.

Bead 2

We're attending a funeral in the same cemetery where our parents have bought their burial plots. After the service they insist we walk over and see. *There's a bench*, says Daddy, *and a shade tree. In case you want to come and visit. Often, I hope.*

She doesn't come often when we are flesh, says Mama, *why would she come when we're just bones?* She rings an arm around mine and we navigate the graves.

> Mama's knees buckle with every step.
> She, who always glided as if on rollerblades.
> Daddy walks ahead, careful not to step
> on the names of the dead.
>
> We goad our parents to lie down.
> And to our surprise, they do.
> Even the sparrows suddenly fall silent
>
> as we lift up our phones to capture
> Mama and Daddy
> practicing their own absence.

Bead 3

Listen,
nothing's too small
for gratitude.

      A midnight touch, a healthy kick
        inside the womb,
teeth in your mouth,
this bowl of steaming rice.

A woman at the village café
watches her daughter sip tea
from a cup round and smooth as her head,
                    chemo-bald,
radiant under the morning sun.

A man pitches his cardboard tent on the side of the road
and pulls a discarded blue quilt up to his chin against the cold.
Another hits a bump in his Tesla
and says *SHIT*, bouncing his children into toothy laughter.

      The woman will take her daughter home,
will kiss her cheeks, still warm.

Say it:
      gratitude.

The cotton sheets, roof, your breath—
crinkled paper napkin on which I write,
      and this cheap pen on its last stretch of ink.

NOTES

FAITH, Bead 8: The three italicized stanzas are the author's translations of passages from Rumi. To locate them in Persian, see Jalāl ad-Dīn Muhammad Rūmī, *Dīvān-e Šhams-e Tabrīzī*, ed. Badiozzaman Forouzanfar (Tehran: University of Tehran Press, 1363 Shamsi), 466; and Jalāl ad-Dīn Muhammad Rūmī, *Dīvān-e Šhams-e Tabrīzī*, ed. Badiozzaman Forouzanfar (Tehran: Amir Kabir Publishers, 1341 Shamsi), 306, 1325.

UN-BLINKING EYES, Bead 2: This poem is for Farah.

HONEYMOON AMONG SARGASSUM: Sargassum is a type of seaweed that inhabits shallow water and coral reefs in the temperate and tropical oceans of the world. Mounds of it arrive each night on the beautiful beaches of Tulum, Mexico. Many upscale resorts in Mexico have their staff dig deep holes in the sand and bury the sargassum at the break of dawn. When the guests come down to breakfast, the beach is spotless, the holes well covered with sand, and the staff busy making breakfast.